SUPER SKILLS

ACTING SKILLS

STEPHANIE TURNBULL

A⁺
Smart Apple Media

Published by Smart Apple Media, an imprint of Black Rabbit Books
P.O. Box 3263, Mankato, Minnesota 56002
www.blackrabbitbooks.com

Printed in the United States of America at Corporate Graphics,
North Mankato, Minnesota

Library of Congress Cataloging-in-Publication Data
Turnbull, Stephanie.
 Acting skills / Stephanie Turnbull.
    p. cm. -- (Super skills)
 Includes index.
 Summary: "Provides readers with acting techniques, presents different kinds
of stage shows, and explains how to create costumes and apply makeup.
Encourages readers to practice acting skills to hone their performance skills.
Lists potential careers that actors and performers have"
--Provided by publisher.
 ISBN 978-1-59920-797-1 (library binding)
 1. Acting--Juvenile literature I. Title.
 PN2061.T87 2012
 792.02'8--dc23
                        2012002527

Created by Appleseed Editions Ltd,
Designed and illustrated by Guy Callaby
Edited by Mary-Jane Wilkins
Photo research by Su Alexander

Picture credits
l = left, r = right, c = center, t = top, b = bottom
page 2t Thinkstock, b Jupiterimages/Thinkstock; 3 Fotosutra.com/Shutterstock; 4
Richard Lewisohn/Thinkstock; 5t Junial Enterprises/Shutterstock, bl Criben/Shutterstock,
br Joe Seer/Shutterstock; 6 Comstock/Thinkstock; 7 Thinkstock; 8 Gary Potts/Shutterstock;
9t Nasgul/Shutterstock, b Ablestock/Thinkstock; 10t Igor Bulgarin/Shutterstock,
c Wikimedia Commons (public domain), b Shutterstock; 11 Shutterstock & Thinkstock;
12 George Muresan/Shutterstock; 13 Thinkstock; 14 Padmayogini/Shutterstock; 15tl
Deklofenak/Shutterstock, tc David Davis/Shutterstock, tr Vibrant Image Studio/
Shutterstock, b Ingvar Bjork/Shutterstock; 16t Harald Hølland Tjøsteim/Shutterstock,
b Stockbyte/Thinkstock; 17 Shutterstock & Thinkstock; 18t Igor Bulgarin/
Shutterstock, c Thinkstock, b·Loke Yek Mang/Shutterstock; 19 Hemera
Technologies/Thinkstock; 20t Hunta/Shutterstock, c Yeko Photo Studios/
Shutterstock, b Carlos Gutierrez/Shutterstock; 22l Osana Perkins/Shutterstock,
r REDAV/Shutterstock; 23 Shutterstock & Thinkstock; 24 Ljupco Smokovski/Shutterstock;
26t Jupiterimages/Thinkstock, b Ariy/Shutterstock; 27t Digital Vision/Thinkstock,
b Jack Q/Shutterstock; 28 Thinkstock; 29tl Shamleen/Shutterstock,
bl Anatema/Shutterstock, tr WithGod/Shutterstock, br Mayskyphoto/
Shutterstock; 30 Digital Vision/Thinkstock; 31 Shutterstock & Thinkstock

Front cover: above Antonin Vodák/Shutterstock, below Stephen Coburn/
Shutterstock

PO1444
2-2012

9 8 7 6 5 4 3 2 1

CONTENTS

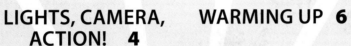

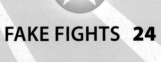

LIGHTS, CAMERA, ACTION!

Have you ever imagined being a famous film star or a great stage actor performing to hundreds of people? Perhaps you enjoy entertaining your friends, or just like the idea of imagining you're someone else. If so, learning to act can be a lot of fun.

▲ Acting in a school play can be a great chance to wear silly costumes and make people laugh!

4

Why Act?

If you're a born performer with lots of energy, acting is a great way of using your talents. If you're shy, acting can help to build your confidence and speaking skills, for example, if you have to give a presentation at school. Acting is a good way of making friends and can be great exercise, too!

▲ *Many people need good speaking skills —for example, lawyers, teachers, and politicians.*

Types of Drama

Actors aim to entertain, but also to educate people or make them think—perhaps about historical events, social issues, or why people behave as they do. Some plays, films, and TV dramas are serious, thrilling, or scary. Others are hilarious; and some are quirky and thoughtful. What kind of drama do you like?

▲ *This zany Spanish play about a wicked plumber and singing, dancing bathroom fixtures teaches children not to waste water.*

SUPER ★ FACTS

★ Perhaps the first-ever actor was Thespis, who lived in ancient Greece and performed in **tragedies**. Because of him, actors are often called thespians.

★ Before the late 17th century, women in many countries weren't allowed to act on stage.

★ Movie actors dream of winning Academy Awards, nicknamed Oscars, which are presented in Hollywood every year.

WARMING UP

Acting involves your whole body and mind. You need to move and speak well and to focus on the character you're trying to be. Here are some great warm-up exercises to prepare your body and your brain.

▲ *Acting involves a lot of teamwork, so do warm-up exercises in a group.*

Loosen Up!

First, relax and forget about everything else in your life. Next, make sure you feel comfortable with other people in the group. Play a game of tag, dance to music, or try one of these exercises.

1. In pairs, crouch low. Slowly and gradually, one person starts moving a part of the body, like a hand, while the other copies, as if creating a mirror image. Keep going, trying to match movements so it isn't obvious who's leading.

This helps you observe and concentrate.

2. Stand in a circle and take turns saying your name followed by an adjective that starts with the same letter or sound, for example, "I am Scott and I am speedy." Then act this out by running in place. Everyone else then does their own "speedy" action.

I am Luke and I am lazy.

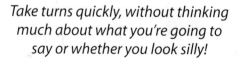
Spend 5 or 10 minutes warming up at the start of every acting session. It really helps!

Take turns quickly, without thinking much about what you're going to say or whether you look silly!

Word Warm-Ups

Actors must speak clearly and loudly enough for everyone to hear. Practice reading a poem or passage from your favorite book to the rest of the group. Loosen up your mouth with tongue twisters, or choose a simple word such as "yes" or "no" and say it in as many different ways as you can.

Voice Exercises

If you're nervous, you may find yourself taking short breaths and gulping for air as you speak. To avoid this, do some controlled breathing exercises.

Yes?

YEEEES!!

1. Stand up straight. Every time you breathe out, try to relax a different body part. Wiggle your shoulders, relax your neck, unclench your jaw, and so on.

2. Put one hand on your stomach. Take a slow, deep breath to make your stomach expand and push your hand forward. Keep your shoulders and chest still. Then breathe out slowly until all the air is gone. Do this a few times.

3. Next, try making a gentle "haaa" sound as you breathe out. Use one whole breath on this sound, opening your mouth wide.

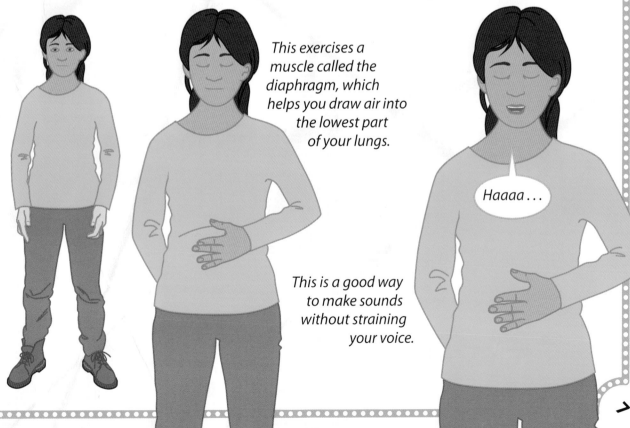

This exercises a muscle called the diaphragm, which helps you draw air into the lowest part of your lungs.

This is a good way to make sounds without straining your voice.

Haaaa . . .

MIME TIME

◀ *Many street performers do mime acts, often wearing masks or white face paint.*

Miming means acting without speaking, using movements to tell stories and show emotions. It's a useful skill as it makes you see how effective gestures can be. It's also a great warm-up exercise.

Yum or Yuck?

Here's a mime game to play with a friend. Sit opposite each other at a table and both imagine a plate of food. Think hard about what the food is and how it smells. Is it delicious, disgusting, or unusual? Now both mime tasting a mouthful. Watch each other's reactions to guess what the food might be!

Whole-Body Mime

Use your whole body to mime some simple actions, such as carrying a tray of hot drinks across a room, unlocking a stuck door, lifting a pile of books, or washing a fragile vase. Again, use your imagination to "see" the objects before you start.

Now try miming in groups. Decide on an object —perhaps a ball, an ice cream cone, or a fluffy chick—then pretend to pass it around.

★ Actors in *Kathakali* theater use mime and dance moves to express feelings and tell stories.

▶ *These modern dancers use mime to strike stylish poses.*

Clowning Around

Clowns and comic actors often use silly, over-the-top mimes, such as trips and falls. Other moves include leaning on an invisible post, fighting against a strong wind, or being trapped in a box. These are harder than they look!

Don't exaggerate your mimes unless you're trying to be funny. And don't make lots of unnecessary moves —standing still can be acting, too.

Funny Stuff

Make your friends laugh by learning some funny mimes. Here's a good one to start with.

1. Go behind a sofa, or a table on its side, and pretend to walk down imaginary steps. Crouch lower with each step, keeping a straight back.

2. Disappear, then come back "up" the steps, carrying something you hid earlier.

CREATING CHARACTERS

Acting means pretending to be someone the audience believes is real. You need to think about every aspect of the person—how they look, move, and speak, as well as how they think, react, and relate to other people. This takes planning and practice.

Pay Attention

Watch professional actors. Choose a character in a film, TV drama, soap opera, or even a commercial and study their expressions, gestures, and way of speaking. Can you believe the character is a real person? Be critical!

▼ *Trying too hard to show emotions can make characters look unrealistic!*

An Acting System

One famous name in acting is the Russian actor and director Constantin Stanislavski (1863–1938). He despaired at the way actors strode on stage and announced their lines to the audience, so he created a system in which actors used their imagination to put themselves in a character's place.

▲ *This is Stanislavski in 1899, acting in a play by Anton Chekhov*

SUPER ★ FACTS

★ Stanislavski began acting when he was seven. He set up his own theater company, the Moscow Art Theater, at 25.

★ Another acting system is method acting. Actors use their own experiences to imagine how characters feel.

Try It Yourself

Use Stanislavski's commonsense system to create a believable character.

1. Try this: In the style of an old person, walk to a chair and sit down. Now think about what you did. Were you bent over, clutching your back with one hand and an imaginary stick with another, looking pained or grumpy?

Is this the character you imagined?

2. Are all old people really like this? Consider an older person you know—a grandparent or neighbor. How do they talk and move? They were young once—can you imagine what they were like?

Looking at old photos may help you.

3. Next, invent the old person you are going to be. Create some background details. Where are you from and what have you done in your life? Are you healthy? What's your attitude to life, and why?

You need peace and quiet to think this through. Try blindfolding yourself to cut out distractions.

4. Now try Stanislavki's "magic if." Imagine how your character would react if certain things happened. For example, what if . . .

. . . you dropped a shopping bag?
. . . you saw a lost dog?
. . . you had a telephone call from an old friend?

5. Still in character, walk to a chair and sit down. This should feel very different from the way you did it in step 1. Now you're acting—not overacting!

Make a habit of observing people. Note mannerisms you could use in characters you invent.

IMPROVISATION

Once you've begun thinking about characters, test your acting skills by **improvising**, or acting out, made-up scenes. These could involve just two people or a larger group. Here are some hints and tips for improvisation.

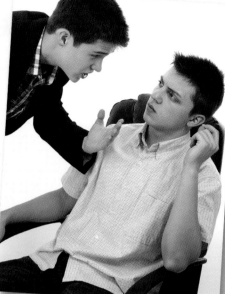

What's the Problem?

An improvised scene doesn't need to be long or complicated, but it must include a problem for characters to explore. For example, two friends waiting for a bus and getting along fine isn't much of a scene. But what if . . .

◀ *Improvising helps you explore how your character might get along with other people.*

. . . they've been waiting for hours?

. . . one person spots something interesting in her friend's bag?

. . . a third, threatening person arrives?

How will your characters deal with the problem? How might the scene develop?

Before you start, look at the checklist on the next page.

IMPROV CHECKLIST

Here's a checklist to consider before you start.

✔ WHO characters are

Decide who your characters are so you know how they will behave.

✔ WHERE the scene takes place

Agree on a setting. A few props such as chairs may be useful. See pages 18–19 for more prop advice.

✔ WHEN the scene takes place

This can affect events a lot—for example, your character could be very grumpy first thing in the morning or scared of the dark.

✔ How the scene BEGINS

Arrange yourselves in a starting position—perhaps you're sitting together, or one person is in the room as the other enters.

✔ How the scene ENDS

Decide on a cue to end the scene —for example, someone says good-bye—or set a timer to ring after a few minutes. Don't worry about trying to resolve the problem or give the scene a neat ending.

Be Inspired

There are many ways of finding improvisation ideas. Think about issues that affect you at home and school, or take a newspaper article and imagine what might happen after the events described. Look at old photos or items in thrift stores and imagine a story based on them. There's also a list of scene ideas on page 30.

Practice a range of scenes, some serious, some light-hearted. Try to avoid getting too silly or **melodramatic** —keep things realistic.

PERFORMING PLAYS

Knowing how to read, learn, and perform a written scene or whole play is a vital acting skill. There are many different types of plays—some funny, tragic, or **satirical**, some with huge **casts** and others for just one person.

▼ *Many plays by William Shakespeare are performed at the Globe Theatre in London.*

Getting Started

First, read the whole **script**, even if you're only performing part of it. Understand the story and find out about the issues it covers and the era it's set in. Look up any words you don't understand. It may also help to see a performance of the play at the theater.

Playing a Part

Take a closer look at your character. Figure out who they are and what they're like. Say your lines out loud. You can only decide how to speak each line once you understand why your character says it. For example, think about different ways these two lines could be spoken.

```
JACK: Where are you going?
JILL: I just need some fresh air.
```

> Where are you going?

> Where are _you_ going?

> Oh, I just need some fresh air!

> Where. Are. You. GOING?

> I-I just need some f-fresh air.

> I just need some fresh _air_, OK?

Is Jack angry, suspicious, surprised, or irritated? Does Jill speak cheerfully, anxiously, impatiently, or sulkily? It all depends on the characters and story.

Teamwork

Next, try acting scenes with all the characters together. This is the tricky part, as it means responding to each other naturally, as if you're having a real conversation rather than reading lines. Consider how fast you're talking. If the scene drags, speed up.

Memory Power

Learning lines can take time, and there's no way around it. Some people copy off lines and stick them around the house to memorize; others record and listen to them on headphones. Don't panic if you have a bad memory. The more you say and think about your lines, the more the words will stick in your mind.

◄ *Photocopy the script and go over your lines with a highlighter.*

When learning lines, look at what other people say, too, otherwise you won't know when it's your turn to speak.

CLEVER COSTUMES

Costumes can help you get into character and make a play look professional. But beware—fussy or badly fitting clothes may get in the way or distract the audience. And never get so obsessed with finding perfect outfits that you forget to rehearse well!

◄ *Elaborate outfits may be hot and heavy to wear.*

Costume Choices

Keep things simple and let the audience use their imagination. A Shakespearian hero doesn't need a full **Elizabethan** outfit—a white shirt and black pants may be fine. Search costume boxes at school and look in thrift stores for useful items.

▲ *You may be able to reuse or adapt an old Halloween costume.*

Be Creative!

Large pieces of material make good, simple costumes. An old sheet or curtain can become a cloak for a soldier . . .

Glue or sew on decorations. Fasten with a brooch or safety pin.

. . . a shawl for a beggar . . .

Cut material to the right size and shape.

. . . or a gown for an alien princess.

Ask creative friends and family to help with sewing, knitting, or altering costumes.

Remember, your audience sees the costume from a distance, so make patterns big and bold.

Making Masks

Wearing a mask is a dramatic way of changing your appearance. If you need to speak, use a half-face mask that won't muffle your voice. Try making masks from card stock or **papier-mâché**.

★ Japanese **Noh** actors wear masks and special symbols to show their character.

★ Old plays are sometimes performed in modern clothes to show that the issues they raise are still important.

★ The most valuable costume from a TV show is a Superman outfit, which was sold in 2003 for more than $123,000

PERFECT PROPS

Props (short for "properties") are objects used by actors. Some are small, handheld items; others are larger things such as tables and chairs. Here are some dos and don'ts for choosing and using props.

◄ *Good props help to set a scene and make characters interesting.*

Keep It Simple

Props are like costumes—the fussier they are, the more problems they can cause. Lots of props create clutter and distract the audience. Small objects may be hard to see from a distance, so unless they're vital to the plot, get rid of them.

Be imaginative —boxes can be chairs, rocks, or castle turrets!

What to Use

Props can be everyday items borrowed from home or school, or bought in thrift stores. Many props in professional plays are specially made, either because they're unusual or because they need to be larger than life for the audience to see. Try making big, bold props using papier-mâché, modeling clay, or cardboard.

Stunt Props

Sometimes props are fake versions of things to avoid injury—for example, swords or other weapons. Fake glass is often made by heating a sugary syrup and leaving it to set hard. It looks and breaks just like glass, which is very useful when an actor has to smash a bottle or plummet through a window!

Fun Fake Blood

Making fake blood to go with stunt props is messy fun! Experiment with the ingredients to get the perfect color.

1. Dollop two large tablespoons of corn syrup into a bowl. Mix in some red food coloring, plus a little yellow to keep the mixture from looking too pink.

▲ *Be sure that your props couldn't really hurt someone!*

3. Dab the mixture on bandages to make them look as though they cover wounds.

Food coloring can stain. Wear an apron and cover the work surface.

2. Mix two teaspoons of instant coffee with a little boiling water and add to darken the mixture. Whisk in a tablespoon of corn starch to thicken your "blood."

AMAZING MAKEUP

Actors in theater, in films, and on TV always wear makeup—sometimes to look natural, sometimes to make a big impact. If you perform on stage, you may need some basic makeup so the audience can see your face clearly.

What to Use

To avoid looking pale and washed out under strong lights, use ordinary makeup to highlight eyes, cheeks, and lips. For a more exaggerated look, try theatrical cosmetics or face paints. Test a small amount on your skin first to check that you aren't allergic to it.

◀ *Stage makeup is bright and bold to show up from a distance.*

Cosmetic Effects

Skilled makeup artists sculpt rubber or plastic to make fake noses, chins, scars, and other features, but you can create dramatic effects without special materials. The key is to use the natural lines and shadows on your face, as shown on the next page.

SUPER ★ FACTS

★ *Early actors coated their faces in a thick, shiny paste called greasepaint.*

★ *Actors in Indian Kathakali theater use makeup to show their characters. A green face means a noble, heroic person, while red signifies evil.*

★ *Today, filmmakers often use computer-generated imagery, or CGI, to create elaborate features instead of using makeup.*

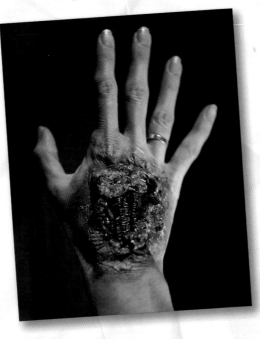

▶ *Soft rubber called latex is molded and painted to create nasty-looking wounds like this.*

Sudden Aging

This is how to make yourself look old.

1. Scrunch up your face and look in a mirror to see where lines and wrinkles form.

2. Go over these lines with dark face paint on a thin brush. Blend the line edges with a finger or a sponge so they don't look like stripes.

Keep your hair out of the way.

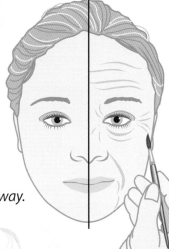

3. Look in the mirror again to see where your skin is darker (under your eyes, on the sides of your nose and below your cheekbones). Put some slightly darker paint on a sponge and dab it on these areas.

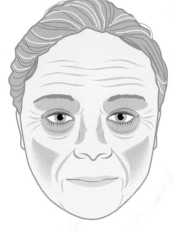

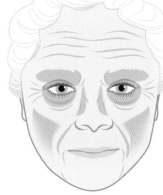

4. Finish the look with a wig, scarf, or hat. You can also buy hair-whitening sprays.

Scary Stuff

Emphasize shadows to create a Halloween-style horror face.

1. First, give yourself a ghostly glow by dabbing on white face paint with a sponge or makeup brush.

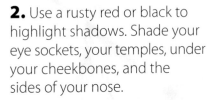

2. Use a rusty red or black to highlight shadows. Shade your eye sockets, your temples, under your cheekbones, and the sides of your nose.

The darker the skin here, the more hollow your cheeks will look.

3. Add details such as eyeliner on eyelids, black lips, a **widow's peak,** and dark, thick eyebrows. You could also dab on fake blood (see page 19).

Look after your skin! Remove makeup afterward, and clean and moisturize your face.

SPECIAL EFFECTS

A few carefully planned special effects, such as dramatic lighting or atmospheric sounds, can make a performance more professional. It also helps to entertain the audience! Here are some hints for creating brilliant special effects.

Stage Lights

If you have lighting equipment, use it, but keep things simple. Bring up lights at the start of a scene and fade them out at the end. Try bringing up lights on different parts of the stage to reveal new characters—or plunge the stage into darkness at an exciting moment.

▲ *Thin plastic sheets called gels are placed over lights to create colors.*

Shadow Fun

Shadows are very effective. Hang a white sheet on a clothesline and shine a bright light behind it. Hold puppets between the sheet and the light to create striking silhouettes.

How about doing a shadow comedy sketch instead? You could pretend to perform a gruesome operation, pulling out fake intestines made of cooked spaghetti or strings of sausages!

Crash! Bang!

You can record sound effects or make them offstage using all kinds of everyday objects. Here are some ideas to get you started.

★ Crumple a potato chip bag or piece of cellophane for a crackling fire sound.

★ Tap together the heels then the toes of a pair of shoes for footsteps.

★ Open and close umbrellas to create the noise of flapping bat wings.

★ Snap a carrot or stick of celery to sound like a bone breaking, or rip apart a crisp head of lettuce for a sickening bone crunch.

How about setting bubble machines around the stage for an underwater or dream scene?

Putting It Together

Here's how to combine lighting and sound (plus great costumes, props, and acting, of course) to create a scene.

1. The stage is dark. A whirring aircraft sound (a fan) gets louder. There is a crash (a box of saucepan lids being plunked down) as the craft lands.

CRASSSH!

2. A spotlight reveals a spaceship. A door swings wide open (a recording of a car trunk opening).

CREEEEEEEK!

3. A robot shuffles out, making metallic blips and buzzes (a recording of a photocopier or printer warming up).

BEEP!

CLICK!

WHIRR!

FAKE FIGHTS

▲ *Convincing fake fights can make serious drama tense and gripping.*

Many professional actors learn how to stage realistic-looking fights. Successful fight moves need good balance, control, teamwork, and lots of practice. Remember that no one should really get hurt!

Don't include fights unless they're important to the plot or in keeping with your characters. If in doubt, leave them out.

Safety First

Always wear comfy clothes, use soft gym mats, and warm up first. Practice in slow motion until you know exactly what you're doing, and never use props such as wooden swords, as they could cause real injuries. If you can, ask an expert to help.

Short and Sweet

Don't be too ambitious. Build up tension and use just a few well-planned moves. If you overdo things, you'll spoil the impact. Here are some actions to try.

Hair Pull

The secret of making this look realistic is that the "victim" does all the work!

1. The attacker and victim stand opposite each other. The attacker clenches a fist, then reaches out and puts it on top of the victim's head as if holding a handful of hair.

2. The victim grabs the fist with both hands and reacts as if he's being pulled around. In fact, he's keeping the attacker's fist in place as he moves.

attacker

victim

Remember to act being angry or in pain.

When the victim is ready to break free, he pushes the attacker's hand away.

Slaps and Punches

1. For a slap, the attacker places the nonhitting hand on the victim's shoulder. This establishes the right distance between them.

2. The attacker moves the non-hitting arm down and swings the other arm back as if it's going to slap the victim. In fact, it goes in front and to the side of the victim.

Exaggerate this swing.

3. As the attacker's arm swings up, the hand slaps the other hand, then follows through with the rest of the swing. The victim reacts to the sound of the slap as if hit.

4. For a fake punch, the attacker uses the same move but swings with a closed fist and smacks it into their other hand.

Falling Down

Here's how to fall safely following a slap or punch.

1. Step backward with one foot. Lower yourself with your weight on the back, bent leg, keeping the front leg almost straight.

2. Sit down and roll backward. Make sure you land slightly to one side, not directly on your spine.

SHOW TIME!

Once you've practiced the skills in this book and learned a play or scene, it's time to go on stage and perform! Here are some tips for using your performance area effectively and making sure everything goes well on opening night.

▲ *Rehearse in your performance area as often as possible, so you know it well.*

Sets and Scenery

Keep your performing area as uncluttered as possible. Stages often have a backdrop you can paint or decorate. Wooden boxes or plastic crates can add varying levels or divide the stage into different areas.

Film a rehearsal to check how a play is progressing. Can you see and hear everyone clearly? Do the props and costumes work? Don't ignore problems—think of ways to solve them.

► *Audiences at this Roman theater sat in a semicircle. Think where your audience will be when you are planning scenery.*

Stage Directions

Many plays give stage directions to tell actors when to enter or exit, or perform certain actions, but you will probably want to add your own moves. Plan these as a group and jot them down on your script in rehearsals to help you remember.

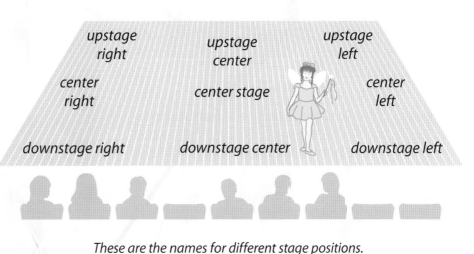

upstage right	upstage center	upstage left
center right	center stage	center left
downstage right	downstage center	downstage left

These are the names for different stage positions. Left and right refer to the actor's view, not the audience's.

The Director

Although acting is about teamwork, it's useful to have a director to take overall charge. Directors decide on stage directions, costumes, props, and scenery. They cut or change long or tricky sections, and advise actors on how to say lines. Good directors are helpful rather than bossy.

◀ *Directors plan the movements and positions of all actors on stage. This is called **blocking**.*

Don't Panic!

It's normal to feel nervous before a performance. Try to relax by giving yourself time to warm up and get into character. Use the breathing exercises on page 7 to help loosen up. If you mess up a line or forget something, try to ignore it and carry on. Keep calm—the audience may not even know you made a mistake.

▲ *Hearing a crowd applaud your performance is a thrilling feeling. Take a bow!*

SUPER ★ FACTS

★ Getting the giggles during a performance is called **corpsing**.

★ To combat **stage fright**, Stanislavski trained actors to concentrate on a small circle that included themselves and one other actor or prop, then gradually widen the circle.

★ It's supposed to be unlucky to wish theater actors good luck, so they say "Break a leg!" instead.

WHAT NEXT?

If you want to be a great actor, the next move is simple: practice! Join drama groups and classes at school or in your area, do quick improvisations with your friends, read plays, and go to the theater.

Go Public

Drama is made to be watched, so don't be shy about performing at school, in local plays, or even in the park. Team up with other talented friends to create a **variety show**. The more you perform, the more confident you'll be. Just make sure you practice well.

Expand Your Skills

Other hobbies can improve your acting and boost your confidence. How about taking singing or music lessons? Learning new art and craft techniques could help you create amazing costumes and scenery.

▲ *Dancing is a great skill, as it keeps you fit and helps you move well on stage.*

◄ *Look for more* Super Skills *books to learn about juggling, tumbling, clowning, puppet making, and many other useful skills!*

An Acting Career

If you're serious about acting as a career, you could study at a special drama school—as long as you pass the **audition** to get in! Remember that an actor's life can be tough. You may work long hours and spend a lot of time away from home with touring plays.

Actors don't get work if they're unreliable or difficult to deal with. Show up on time, listen to directions, and learn to deal with criticism.

Who knows where your acting interests will take you? Related careers include (clockwise from above) camera operator, stunt performer, DJ, and puppeteer!

More Job Ideas

Acting isn't the only job you can do in the world of performing arts. How about becoming a scriptwriter, director, stand-up comedian, or magician? Maybe you could train as a TV presenter, prop maker, lighting technician, or **voice-over artist**.

GLOSSARY

audition
A test to show your acting talents.

blocking
Planning out the movements and positions of the actors on stage.

cast
All the actors in a play or other performance.

Elizabethan
From the reign of Queen Elizabeth I (1558–1603). Plays were very popular at this time, including many by the famous writer William Shakespeare.

improvising
Performing with little or no planning beforehand, making things up as you go along.

Kathakali
Traditional Indian drama that includes dance and mime.

melodramatic
Exaggerated and over the top, with extreme, unrealistic characters and emotions.

Noh
Traditional Japanese drama that includes dance and song.

papier-mâché
Bits of paper mixed with glue and molded into a shape that dries hard.

satirical
Drama that uses satire, which is a way of criticizing people or ideas by making them look silly.

script
A printed copy of all the spoken words and stage directions to be used in a play or other performance.

stage fright
Nervousness or panic about performing in public.

tragedy
A serious play that ends with disaster.

variety show
A performance made up of different acts, such as songs, dances, comedy sketches, and circus or magic routines.

voice-over artist
Someone who speaks on a film, TV show, or commercial but isn't seen on screen.

widow's peak
A v-shaped point of hair in the middle of the forehead.

Extra Improvisation Scenes

Here are some ideas for more improvisations. They each involve two characters, but you could include more people. Pick one and talk it over for a few minutes, considering the points on the checklist on page 13, then try acting it.

★ A girl decides to tell her mother about a problem at school.

★ A newspaper reporter asks a lottery winner for an interview.

★ Two friends hear a thump on the roof while babysitting.

★ A customer in a restaurant calls the waiter over to complain.

★ A traveler at an airport makes a confession to a stranger.

★ A father sees his son getting out of a police car.

★ A teenager notices an elderly lady dropping something.

★ A girl on vacation spots someone she knows from school.

★ A woman walking home thinks she's being followed.

★ Two people who hate each other get stuck in an elevator together.

USEFUL WEBSITES

www.acting-school-stop.com
This large website offers online acting lessons and videos, plus
helpful hints for acting on screen, doing voice-overs, and much more.

www.collegegrad.com/careers/proft.23.shtml
or
www.bls.gov/oco/ocos093.htm
Find all kinds of useful, practical information about becoming an actor,
including advice on studying, job opportunities, and related careers.

www.ehow.com/search.html?q=theatrical+make-up&skin=corporate&t=video
Watch lots of videos showing clever stage makeup techniques.

www.helium.com/knowledge/53773-acting-how-to-learn-lines
Read articles written by actors suggesting good ways of learning lines.

www.theaternewsonline.com
Read theater reviews, listings, articles, and blogs in this
online entertainment newspaper.

www.epicsound.com/sfx/index.php
Scroll through a fascinating list of sound effect ideas
submitted by sound designers from around the world.
Some are simple enough to try yourself, while others
need complicated equipment.